D1547613

The Choice Vine: Mary Magdalene, the Sacred Whore, and the Benjamite Inheritance

By Tracy R. Twyman

ISBN: 978-1-962312-22-6

Originally published with
Dagobert's Revenge Magazine © 2003

The Choice Vine: Mary Magdalene, the Sacred Whore, and the Benjamite Inheritance
By Tracy R. Twyman

*Originally published with Dagobert's Revenge Magazine ©
2003*

*Who was Mary Magdalene? Is it true that she was married
to Jesus? If so, why did he choose her?*

This groundbreaking work by Tracy R. Twyman
(Dagobert's Revenge, Merovingian Mythos, etc.) explores
the royal heritage of Mary Magdalene in the Tribe of
Benjamin. The connections between the Benjamites, Baal-
worship, sex rituals, and the Merovingian bloodline are
revealed.

Is it possible that Jesus and Mary Magdalene were part of a
sacred sex cult with its roots in the ancient world? Could
they both have been descended from a royal race of sex
gods from the heavens? Discover the clues pieced together
by Tracy R. Twyman in The Choice Vine , available from
Quintessential Publications.

Table of Contents

Jesus and Mary Magdalene

The Smear Campaign

Due to the recent popularity of *The Da Vinci Code*, as well as the rising tide of Wicca, New Age, and "goddess worship" that we have seen over the last few years, the subject of Mary Magdalene has been quite fashionable as of late. She has been covered in *Time Magazine*, *Newsweek*, on The History Channel, the Learning Channel, PAX, and in specials aired on all the major networks. *The Gospel of Mary Magdalene* has ranked Amazon.com's top 100, as has Lynn Picknett's *Mary Magdalene*, and Margaret Starbird's *The Woman with the Alabaster Jar* - a book first published in 1993, and one of the major influences on Dan Brown's *The Da Vinci Code*. The idea that the Magdalene may have actually been the bride of Christ and the mother of his children is now one that is taken quite seriously amongst the general public, as is the theory that they were the progenitors of the Merovingian kings of France - the so-called "Grail bloodline." The circulation of these ideas has caused an interest in occult spiritual matters to blossom in a sudden and unexpected way, and appears to be setting off the "Arcadian revival" about which we at *Dagobert's Revenge* have prophesized for many years.

But along with this interest has come speculation about the reasons why Jesus' marriage to Mary Magdalene was not written of in the Gospels, or anywhere in the canonized New Testament. The question is, "Why did the Church edit Christ's wife out of the Bible?" Lead by the Wiccans, the New Agers, and the Feminists, many have leapt to the conclusion that this was the result of a misogynist conspiracy by the male-dominated Catholic Church. According to this line of thought, Church doctrine held human sexuality to be sinful because of an institutional hatred which held women to be inherently corrupt. They therefore did not want to admit that Christ had any wives or children, but maintained that he had remained chaste his whole life, as had his Virgin mother. The Gospels and the Church also suppressed any knowledge of the high-ranking positions that Mary and other women held in the Jesus movement.

It certainly is true that the Roman Church hierarchy and doctrine was misogynist in nature, but then again so was the rest of the world. It also does seem that the Jesus movement was, in comparison, relatively enlightened in this regard. However, the severe doctoring and suppression that was done by the Church to the historical records of Jesus and his family indicate more than just misogyny. The Church established the doctrine of the "virgin birth" to disconnect Jesus from the genealogy of his father, Joseph, a descendant of King David, and for a while tried to maintain that the Virgin Mary had herself been conceived in the same manner, thus disconnecting Jesus from her side of the family as well. They tried to establish the *perpetual* virginity of Mary, thus claiming that Jesus had no biological brothers or sisters, and maintained that the many "brothers" of Jesus mentioned in the Gospels were either children of Joseph from a previous marriage, or merely "brothers in spirit." They then insisted that Jesus had remained chaste his entire life as well. The numerous passages in the Bible proclaiming Jesus as "King of the Jews," "the son of David," and "the Messiah" (a title bestowed traditionally upon the rightful king of Judah) have all been held by the Church to be metaphorical. Christ's real kingdom is in Heaven, the Church has always maintained - not in Israel. Pilate referred to Jesus as "King of the Jews" *mockingly*, they say. After all, how could he literally be king when he had no ancestors, no father, no brothers, no wife, and no heirs? Thus began a smear campaign and a genocidal persecution that has continued for approximately 2000 years.

The real reason why Mary Magdalene was "written out of the Bible," and otherwise maligned by the Church, was because she was evidence of the continuation of Jesus' royal line. Furthermore, *who she really was* indicated the true meaning of Jesus' mission. If the truth about Jesus' marriage to Mary were known, the entire edifice of Rome's doctrine may very well come tumbling down.

A Benjamite Queen

In *The Woman with the Alabaster Jar*, Margaret Starbird theorizes that little may be known of the marriage partially because it may have purposely been kept secret by Jesus and his closest followers. According to Starbird, this was a direct result of the royal nature of the union. It was, she says, a "dynastic alliance." She, like many others, believes that "Mary Magdalene" and "Mary of Bethany" were the same person, and writes:

I have come to suspect that Jesus had a secret dynastic
marriage with Mary of Bethany, and that she was a
daughter of the tribe of Benjamin, whose ancestral heritage
was the land surrounding the Holy City of David, the city
Jerusalem. A dynastic marriage between Jesus and a royal
daughter of the Benjamites would have been perceived as
asource of healing to the people of Israel during their time
of misery as an occupied nation.

Numerous researchers have connected Magdalene to the tribe of
Benjamin, which provided Israel with its first king, Saul. Although
Saul was soon deposed by David, a descendant of Judah (a tribe
whom God himself had sanctioned to provide the kings of Israel),
the tribes of Judah and Benjamin maintained a close relationship
with the Benjamites, eventually becoming subsumed into the tribe
of Judah. (More will be said on this subject later on.) As noted by
Starbird, the city of Jerusalem itself was technically a Benjamite
city, although the kings of Judah maintained it as their royal
capitol. Benjamin (which means "son of the right hand" in
Hebrew) was the youngest of Jacob's twelve sons, so for this tribe
to provide Israel's first king, as well as the Messiah's heir (through
the Magdalene), would have been a great example of how, as Jesus
himself states in the Gospels, "the last shall be the first, and the
first shall be the last." But that is not all of the inheritance that a
Benjamite princess like Magdalene might bring to the table. There
are many other layers of meaning to her symbolic value.

When Jacob was lying on his deathbed, he handed out blessings
and curses to each of his sons, as was the tradition at that time. And
even though God himself had established the tradition that men
should pass on the greatest portion of their inheritance to their
firstborn son, with the Biblical patriarchs that rarely turned out to
be the case, as the elder son was almost always disqualified for
some reason or another. Thus, essentially skipping over his first
three sons (who were cursed for actions they had taken earlier in

life), Jacob placed the bulk of his blessing on his forth son Judah, to whom he said:

> Judah, thou art he whom thy brethren shall praise: thy hand shall be in the neck of thine enemies; thy father's children shall bow down before thee. Judah is a lion's whelp: from the prey, my son, thou art gone up: he stooped down, he couched as a lion, and as an old lion; who shall rouse him up? The scepter shall not depart from Judah, nor a lawgiver from between his feet, until Shiloh come; and unto him shall the gathering of the people be. Binding his foal unto the vine, and his ass's colt unto the choice vine; he washed his garments in wine, and his clothes in the blood of grapes: His eyes shall be red with wine, and his teeth white with milk. *(Genesis 49:8-12.)*

Meanwhile, to Benjamin, Jacob said the following:

> Benjamin shall ravin as a wolf: in the morning he shall devour the prey, and at night he shall divide the spoil. (*Genesis* 49:27.)

Author Olaf Hage, on his website Hage Productions has written an article interpreting these words and what they say about Mary Magdalene. He sees Magdalene as a Benjamite princess, with an important dynastic inheritance stemming from her father, Simon the Leper. Olfa Hage also equates Simon with another character from the Gospels as well: Nicodemus, one of the Sanhedrin council members, and the one who anoints (or prepares to anoint) Jesus' body for burial after his crucifixion, according to the Gospels. As Hage writes:

> The house of Benjamin was given the right to keep the written genealogies of the priests and kings, to decide which persons were entitled to inherit. The Torah says Benjamin will 'Divide the spoils' that is, the inheritance of

Israel... But the tribe of Benjamin could do more than keep written records that designated the Priest and King. It could anoint them.

This point addresses the scene in the Gospels which has earned Mary her association with her alabaster jar - her anointing of the head and feet of Jesus with spikenard. *Matthew 26:6-13* states:

> Now when Jesus was in Bethany, in the house of Simon the leper, There came unto him a woman having an alabaster box of very precious ointment, and poured it on his head, as he sat at meat. But when his disciples saw it, they had indignation, saying, To what purpose is this waste? For this ointment might have been sold for much, and given to the poor. When Jesus understood it, he said unto them, Why trouble ye the woman? for she hath wrought a good work upon me. For ye have the poor always with you; but me ye have not always. For in that she hath poured this ointment on my body, she did it for my burial. Verily I say unto you, Wheresoever this gospel shall be preached in the whole world, there shall also this, that this woman hath done, be told for a memorial of her.[1]

According to Olaf Hage:

> When Mary brought out the 'genuine nard' and anointed Jesus, she was declaring Jesus the official king... This act of hers... is standard practice for an official royal anointing.

Margaret Starbird concurs, and adds:

> ... in more ancient times, the anointing of the sacred king was the unique privilege of a royal bride. For millennia this

---

[1] It is interesting that this anointing oil is considered symbolic of the anointments that would later be used by Nicodemus (Magdalene's father, according to Olaf Hage) to actually anoint Jesus' dead body.

same action has been part of an actual marriage rite, performed by a daughter of the royal house, and the marriage rite itself conferred kingship upon her consort.

Starbird echoes a theme that has been suggested by many authors before: that Jesus' church was, at the highest level, a Greco-Roman-Judaic mystery cult, in which Mary Magdalene performed the role of the Sacred Prostitute. She writes:

> The anointing performed by the woman at Bethany was similar to the familiar ritual practice of a sacred priestess or temple 'prostitute' in the Goddess cults of the Roman Empire. Even the term 'prostitute' is a misnomer. This term, chosen by modern translators, is applied to the hierodilae, or 'sacred woman' of the temple... At some periods of Jewish history, they were even a part of the ritual worship in the Temple of Jerusalem...

The Alchemical Wedding

Seen in this light, the wedding of Jesus and Mary, which many people see as being represented in the Gospels by the story of the wedding at Cana, becomes nothing less than a Gnostic sex magic ritual, and Mary's anointing of Jesus was an integral part of it. Starbird continues:

> The anointing of the head had erotic significance, the head being symbolic of the phallus 'anointed' by the woman for penetration during the physical consummation of marriage... Through this union with the priestess, the king/consort received royal status. He became known as the 'Anointed One' - in Hebrew, the 'Messiah.'

Other writers concur that Mary Magdalene was a temple priestess or "sacred prostitute" for Jesus' cult, and that she acted in this regard as Jesus' "Grail Maiden." Nicholas de Vere, in his book *The*

Dragon Legacy: The Secret History of an Ancient Bloodline, states his opinion that the main sex magic ritual which was engaged in by this cult was the non-penetrative ritual of "Starfire," in which a mixture of menstrual blood and female ejaculate is consumed by the priest directly from the vagina of the priestess. It is consumed, says De Vere, because if the priestess is of the "Grail bloodline," these fluids will contain the "Philosopher's Stone" (a.k.a. "Ormus,""Occultum," or "monatomic [white powder] gold") - special secretions from the pineal gland found, he says, more concentratedly in the fluids of Grail bloodline members. If the priest is of the bloodline as well, as Jesus would have been, consuming these fluids would initiate a transcendental spiritual experience for the priest, and to a lesser extent, for any participating "guests" at the "wedding." This is the capacity in which Magdalene would have served as a "priestess" or "Grail maiden," and according to De Vere, she would have begun doing so at a very young age:

> She was twelve at the time and he was, according to the Bible, about thirty years old. The ritual employed was similar to that in which Lazarus partook, in that it involved symbolic death and resurrection. (See *Luke 8*: verse 41-56.) Following her initiation and during the period of her adolescence, as was common practice, Mary would have acted as Jesus' handmaiden or grail priestess.

De Vere claims that this was part of a family tradition for the member's of Jesus' cult, most of whom were biologically related to him. He believes Jesus' mother was a priestess as well:

> Both Jesus' mother Mary and his wife Mary Magdalene were called the 'crystal wombs from which shined forth the light of God,' a description which suggests strongly the Tantric and Qabalistic concept of Starfire.

Something along these lines does seem to be indicated symbolically in the story of the wedding at Cana - Christ and Magdalene's wedding, according to some. The transformation of water into wine seems to point to an alchemical ritual, which sex magic certainly is, in which the water and wine could refer to female ejaculate and menstrual blood (respectively), particularly given the symbolism of Mary and her bloodline as "the choice vine."

Indeed, such a symbolic connection appears to be made in *The Song of Solomon*, which is a coded document describing a royal sex magic ritual performed by the Judaic King Solomon (Jesus' ancestor and predecessor), with one of his many wives or concubines. Human body fluids like vaginal secretions, female ejaculate, semen, menstrual blood, and other things, such as sexual organs, are disguised as "spikenard," "wine," "myrrh," "living waters," "the Rose of Sharon," and "the Lily of the Valley." Quotes from the poem such as the following have, understandably, been interpreted as a sexual manner:

- "Because of the savour of thy good ointments thy name is as ointment poured forth, therefore do the virgins love thee."

- "While the king sitteth at his table, my spikenard sendeth forth the smell thereof."

- "Thy lips, O my spouse, drop as the honeycomb: honey and milk are under thy tongue; and the smell of thy garments is like the smell of Lebanon."

- "Thy plants are an orchard of pomegranates, with pleasant fruits; camphire, with spikenard..."

- "I sleep, but my heart waketh: it is the voice of my beloved that knocketh, saying, Open to me, my sister, my love, my dove, my undefiled: for my head is filled with dew, and my locks with the drops of the night. I have put off my coat;

how shall I put it on? I have washed my feet; how shall I defile them?"

- "I rose up to open to my beloved; and my hands dropped with myrrh, and my fingers with sweet smelling myrrh, upon the handles of the lock."

- "I would lead thee, and bring thee into my mother's house, who would instruct me: I would cause thee to drink of spiced wine of the juice of my pomegranate."

Interestingly, the "bride" in this poem describes herself symbolically as "black," just as Mary Magdalene was represented in some European churches as the "Black Madonna." (I will get back to the symbolism of this in due course.) The poem states:

Look not upon me, because I am black, because the sun hath looked upon me: my mother's children were angry with me; they made me the keeper of the vineyards; but mine own vineyard have I not kept.

Interestingly, Solomon refers to his bride as his "sister" in this poem. Sex magic rituals are, at root, a reenactment of an ancient god (equivalent to the Egyptian Osiris) mating with his ancient consort (equivalent to the Egyptian Isis), and in many versions of this myth, including the Egyptian, these two are brother and sister. This would make sense if they were practicing royal sex magic, as Nicholas de Vere describes it, in which the participants are sharing sacred essences inherent in their divine blood. De Vere, like other writers before him, has chosen to analyze the hierogamy purportedly practiced by Jesus and Mary Magdalene in terms of the imagery of *The Song of Solomon*. He writes:

...In this manner, Mary means 'spirit in the womb' or 'womb-fire.' It is in the latter instance that we have a direct reference to the Tantric Kaula ritual of enlivening or inflaming the chakra of the uterine region to produce the 'waters of life' or, as *The Song of Solomon* puts it, 'The well of living waters.' Marys symbol is the white lily of the valley, the fleur-de-lys. As the 'Well of living waters,' Mary's relationship to Jesus becomes clearer as the child handmaiden of the Messach, the Dragon God-King. 'Marie' is an ancient form of the word 'marry,' meaning 'to join to unite with,' as in alchemical marriage, divine enthea, hierogamy, the sacred marriage ritual of Solomon's Song...'

In the ancient traditions of hierogamy, or royal sex magic, the "wedding" takes place just prior to the sacrifice of the "sacred king" (symbolized by the high priest), and the sex ritual anointed him as king, just in time for his ritual death. This was the case in the ancient fertility cults, in which the death of the king ensured agricultural prosperity, and this was the case with Mary and Jesus. In Matthew's version of the anointing ceremony, which was part of the sacred marriage act, it was followed immediately by Judas' betrayal, which leads to Jesus' sacrifice on the cross. Jesus even stated explicitly that she was anointing him for his burial. This would make Mary a participant in the ritual slaying of Jesus. Nicholas de Vere sees this as being part of the symbolic ceremony, and apparently does not believe that Jesus was actually slain in the flesh. He writes:

After Jesus' death, Magdalene went to the cell and found it open. Rather, I would argue that in accordance with the traditional ritual that accompanied her station, she was expected to stay in the cell and commune with the Ka of Jesus in the Underworld. Few people actually knew the real reason why she went... That she went to heal him of his non-fatal wounds was a secret known only to an initiated few, among whom the apostles, it seems, were not counted.

Of the function of Grail maidens in general, De Vere has this to say:

The girls, whose watery embrace is said to spell death, are the Shunnamites, the lilies or virgins who are portrayed in *The Song of Solomon*. In their connection with water, the nymphs are thus depicted as the embodiment of the wells of living waters. Their deathly embrace is but the death of the ego, of the will, and of desire.

Others concur about the connection between sex and death in this sacred kingship ritual. Margaret Starbird writes that that sacred marriage "includes the torture and death of the anointed Bridegroom/King." Likewise, in an article on lost-civilizations.net, entitled "The Horse Sacrifice," the unnamed author writes about a ritual:

> ... celebrated in Sumer and Babylon on the occasion of the New Year Festival (Akitu). In this ritual, the king would ritually mate with a sacred prostitute (hierodule) inside a shrine on top of the ziggurat. This building, a sort of stepped pyramid, represented the Cosmic Mountain, itself a replica of the Cosmos. Hence, the couple united inside the temple or the altar represented the Primordial Couple buried inside the Cosmic Mountain, in Paradise. Very likely, the Heb Sed festival of the Egyptians, as well as the secret ceremonies celebrated inside the Egyptian temples and pyramids, were also ritual enactments of the Cosmogonic Hierogamy, the Sacred Marriage of the King and the Sacred Prostitute, the Hierodule of Bastit or of some other similar goddess ... In the ashvamedha, the wife of the officiating priest the mahishi simulated a ritual mating with the sacrificial horse. The mahishi (lit. "the Great Cow") represented the Earth, much as the horse symbolized the Sun. Indeed, she also stood for the queen as the Primordial Whore, just as her husband (the mahisha) was an alias of the Horse, the Sun, the Primordial Male (or buffalo). The couple stood for Heaven and Earth and, more

exactly, for Yama and Yami, the Primordial Couple of paradisial times.

It is looking more and more like Jesus' wedding was the most important aspect of his life, his ministry, and his political bid for the kingship of Israel - more so even than his death. In fact, his death looks more and more like it was symbolic, and that he did not really die, but rather was pretending to be sacrificed as part of an ancient ritual of marriage, death, and rebirth, the act of which turned him from a priest and a prophet into a god-king: the Messiah. Mary's association with the color black can be considered an extension of her embodiment of the archetype of Isis, the "black widow" who was symbolically veiled in black as she mourned for her dead husband, Osiris. The color black represents, in alchemy, the "nigrido," the prima materia from whence the Philosopher's Stone is made. This is also called the "death phase" in alchemy, and is further symbolized by a dead king (drowned or decapitated), or by a skull (like the one Mary Magdalen is almost always depicted with).

Although De Vere's theory may be correct, in that there was no penetrative intercourse, but only the consumption of body fluids, there may indeed have been intercourse as well, resulting in a child - a royal heir and son (or daughter) of God (at least symbolically). If there were such a child, it would be born after Jesus' symbolic death, and would be a "widow's son." This is the term used to identify Horus in the Rites of Isis, who was conceived when Isis mated with the dead body of Osiris. This she accomplished by putting together all of the pieces of Osiris' body (which his brother Set had chopped to bits), and providing a substitute for the one missing piece: his penis. This story is a disguised account of a sex magic ritual in which the priest is possessed by the spirit of Osiris, and acts as a "substitute penis" so that the dead god can impregnate the young priestess and breed a royal heir. The term "widow's son" has significance in the rites of Freemasonry, where it is applied to

Hiram, the builder of Solomon's Temple, and all Freemasons refer to themselves metaphorically as "widow's sons." Also, in the Gospels, there is a story in which Jesus raises from the dead a man described as a "son of a widow." This tale clearly describes in metaphor yet another death and resurrection ritual performed by the cult of Christ. Jesus himself was undoubtedly conceived during one of these rituals, which may account for the purportedly divine nature of his conception.

From Jesus' own words, we glean that his entire ministry, and the "kingdom of heaven" itself, could be thought of as a "wedding," while the "church" which he was raising up was his "bride." This is how the Roman Catholic and Protestant Christian churches have chosen to interpret the numerous metaphorical references Jesus made to "the wedding," "the marriage," the "bride" and the "bridegroom." In *Matthew 9:15*, we read:

> And Jesus said unto them, Can the children of the bridechamber mourn, as long as the bridegroom is with them? but the days will come, when the bridegroom shall be taken from them, and then shall they fast.

Later, in *Matthew, 25:1-13*, Jesus tells a fascinating parable indicating that only the chosen few will be able to participate as brides in this "wedding":

> Then shall the kingdom of heaven be likened unto ten virgins, which took their lamps, and went forth to meet the bridegroom. And five of them were wise, and five were foolish. They that were foolish took their lamps, and took no oil with them: But the wise took oil in their vessels with their lamps. While the bridegroom tarried, they all slumbered and slept. And at midnight there was a cry made, Behold, the bridegroom cometh; go ye out to meet him. Then all those virgins arose, and trimmed their lamps. And the foolish said unto the wise, Give us of your oil; for our

lamps are gone out. But the wise answered, saying, Not so;
lest there be not enough for us and you: but go ye rather to
them that sell, and buy for yourselves. And while they went
to buy, the bridegroom came; and they that were ready
went in with him to the marriage: and the door was shut.
Afterward came also the other virgins, saying, Lord, Lord,
open to us. But he answered and said, Verily I say unto you,
I know you not. Watch therefore, for ye know neither the
day nor the hour wherein the Son of man cometh.

And earlier in the same book, Jesus indicates that even the guest
list at this "wedding" will be selective:

The kingdom of heaven is like unto a certain king, which
made a marriage for his son. And sent forth his servants to
call them that were bidden to the wedding: and they would
not come. Again, he sent forth other servants, saying, Tell
them which are bidden, Behold, I have prepared my dinner:
my oxen and my fatlings are killed, and all things are
ready: come unto the marriage. But they made light of it,
and went their ways, one to his farm, another to his
merchandise: And the remnant took his servants, and
entreated them spitefully, and slew them.

But when the king heard thereof, he was wroth: and he sent
forth his armies, and destroyed those murderers, and burned
up their city. Then saith he to his servants, The wedding is
ready, but they which were bidden were not worthy. Go ye
therefore into the highways, and as many as ye shall find,
bid to the marriage.

So those servants went out into the highways, and gathered
together all as many as they found, both bad and good: and
the wedding was furnished with guests. And when the king
came in to see the guests, he saw there a man which had not
on a wedding garment: And he saith unto him, Friend, how

camest thou in hither not having a wedding garment? And he was speechless.

Then said the king to the servants, Bind him hand and foot, and take him away, and cast him into outer darkness, there shall be weeping and gnashing of teeth. For many are called, but few are chosen.

The wedding at Cana, possibly that of Jesus and Mary Magdalene

In *Luke 12:36*, Jesus tells his disciples to be "like unto men that wait for their lord, when he will return from the wedding; that when he cometh and knocketh, they may open unto him immediately." And in *Luke 14:8* he warns them: "When thou art bidden of any [man] to a wedding, sit not down in the highest room; lest a more honourable man than thou be bidden of him..." In *John 3:39*, he tells his followers to be glad, even if they are not lucky enough to marry themselves, just to be able to witness the wedding:

> He that hath the bride is the bridegroom: but the friend of the bridegroom, which standeth and heareth him, rejoiceth greatly because of the bridegroom's voice: this my joy therefore is fulfilled.

In this light, the symbol of the Rose-Croix can be seen to represent the marriage of Christ (symbolized by the cross) and the Magdalene (symbolized by the rose, as she is to this very day). Though its roots are far more ancient than the time of Jesus (as it symbolized the primordial concept of the sexual union of god and goddess which Jesus and Mary were themselves trying to emulate), the Rosicrucians, themselves initiates into the true mysteries of Christ, may have been directly referencing this particular alchemical wedding when they employed this symbol. This theory may bring us a new interpretation of the classic Rosicrucian text, *The Chemical Wedding of Christian Rosenkreutz*. In this story, the narrator is cordially invited (by an angel, no less) to a royal wedding with a very exclusive guest list. The path to get to the wedding is treacherous and difficult. Rosenkreutz is tested on wisdom and purity of heart several times at the gate to the castle, and again at the door, and must even purchase a special token to gain admittance. Once he is arrived, there are further tests, and several of the guests are eliminated. The goings-on of the wedding are very peculiar, mystical, and shrouded in metaphor - the typically impenetrable maze of alchemical allegory. The ceremony takes place over several days, and includes the death and rebirth of the king. It would be easy to see this text as an allegory for Jesus and Mary's ritual wedding. At one point during the narrator's stay at the castle, he stumbles upon the tomb of the "sleeping Lady Venus." As he describes it:

> The sepulcher was triangular, and had in the middle of it a kettle of polished copper... In the kettle stood an angel, who held in his arms an unknown tree, from which it continually dropped fruit into the kettle; and as oft as the fruit fell into the kettle, it turned into water, and ran out from thence into three small golden kettles standing by.

On the bed of the Lady Venus he finds a tablet upon which is written:

> When the fruit of my tree shall be quite melted down, then I shall awake and be the mother of a king.

In *The Dragon Legacy: The Secret History of an Ancient Bloodline*, Nicholas de Vere analyzes several similar allegorical tales and legends involving trees that drop fruit into pools. About them, collectively, he has this to say:

> The well... [symbolizes] the womb and the vagina, below which is the vulva, the tree growing next to the well represents the lower and upper torso, the head and the arms of the virgin female. The twigs and branches of the tree symbolize the veins and arteries of rich, Holy Royal Blood, and the fruits of the tree represent the endocrinal glands that correspond to the chakras in Tantrism...

The Curse of the Benjamites

So was Mary Magdalene a "sex goddess"? According to my research, she was. Moreover, her descent from the tribe of Benjamin may have made her particularly qualified for the role. This pertains to a peculiar story regarding this tribe that can be found at the end of *The Book of Judges*. In Chapter 19 of that book, we read:

> And it came to pass in those days, when there was no king in Israel, that there was a certain Levite sojourning on the side of mount Ephraim, who took to him a concubine out of Bethlehemjudah. And his concubine played the whore against him, and went away from him unto her father's house to Bethlehemjudah, and was there four whole months. And her husband arose, and went after her, to speak friendly unto her, and to bring her again, having his servant with him, and a couple of asses: and she brought him into her father's house: and when the father of the damsel saw him, he rejoiced to meet him. (*Judges* 19:1-3.)

The Levite and his wife/concubine spend several days at their father-in-law's house, and then begin their journey back to their home in Bethlehemjudah. On the way back it begins to get dark, so they decide to sojourn for the night in the Benjamite city of Gibeah. But no one there would take them into their house, so they sat down in the street, determined to sleep there. Then an old man who lived there came across to them:

> And when he had lifted up his eyes, he saw a wayfaring man in the street of the city: and the old man said, Whither goest thou? and whence comest thou? And he said unto him, We are passing from Bethlehemjudah toward the side of mount Ephraim; from thence am I: and I went to Bethlehemjudah, but I am now going to the house of the LORD; and there is no man that receiveth me to house. Yet there is both straw and provender for our asses; and there is bread and wine also for me, and for thy handmaid, and for the young man which is with thy servants: there is no want of any thing. And the old man said, Peace be with thee; howsoever let all thy wants lie upon me; only lodge not in the street. So he brought him into his house, and gave

provender unto the asses: and they washed their feet, and did eat and drink. (*Judges* 19:17-21.)

It is at this point that our story takes a turn for the stranger. The house is besieged by a group of Benjamites referred to as "sons of Belial," seeking to commit lewd acts of sodomy with the young Levite. As the text states:

Now as they were making their hearts merry, behold, the men of the city, certain sons of Belial, beset the house round about, and beat at the door, and spake to the master of the house, the old man, saying, Bring forth the man that came into thine house, that we may know him.

And the man, the master of the house, went out unto them, and said unto them, Nay, my brethren, nay, I pray you, do not so wickedly; seeing that this man is come into mine house, do not this folly. Behold, here is my daughter a maiden, and his concubine; them I will bring out now, and humble ye them, and do with them what seemeth good unto you: but unto this man do not so vile a thing. But the men would not hearken to him: so the man took his concubine, and brought her forth unto them; and they knew her, and abused her all the night until the morning: and when the day began to spring, they let her go.

Then came the woman in the dawning of the day, and fell down at the door of the man's house where her lord was, till it was light. And her lord rose up in the morning, and opened the doors of the house, and went out to go his way: and, behold, the woman his concubine was fallen down at the door of the house, and her hands were upon the threshold. And he said unto her, Up, and let us be going. But none answered. Then the man took her up upon an ass, and the man rose up, and gat him unto his place. (*Judges* 19:22-28.)

You would think that the Levite had known, when the old man offered his concubine up to be raped by the sons of Belial, that something bad was going to happen to her, and thus he should not have been surprised to find her dead the next day. If he had any objection to this, one would think that he would have stopped the old man from offering her up. Yet he does not seem terribly upset, but nonetheless sets about to take revenge, by dividing his concubine's body into twelve parts, and sending one to each of the tribes of Israel! Presumably he did this as a way of informing them about the injustice that was done to him, to seek their help in avenging her death. The text reads:

> And when he was come into his house, he took a knife, and laid hold on his concubine, and divided her, together with her bones, into twelve pieces, and sent her into all the coasts of Israel. And it was so, that all that saw it said, There was no such deed done nor seen from the day that the children of Israel came up out of the land of Egypt unto this day: consider of it, take advice, and speak your minds. (*Judges* 19:29-30.)

Then, all eleven of the other tribes agreed to wage war against the entire tribe of Benjamin, for allowing this injustice to take place in their territory:

> Then all the children of Israel went out, and the congregation was gathered together as one man, from Dan even to Beersheba, with the land of Gilead, unto the LORD in Mizpeh. And the chief of all the people, even of all the tribes of Israel, presented themselves in the assembly of the people of God, four hundred thousand footmen that drew sword.
>
> (Now the children of Benjamin heard that the children of Israel were gone up to Mizpeh.) Then said the children of Israel, Tell us, how was this wickedness? And the Levite,

the husband of the woman that was slain, answered and said, I came into Gibeah that belongeth to Benjamin, I and my concubine, to lodge. And the men of Gibeah rose against me, and beset the house round about upon me by night, and thought to have slain me: and my concubine have they forced, that she is dead. And I took my concubine, and cut her in pieces, and sent her throughout all the country of the inheritance of Israel: for they have committed lewdness and folly in Israel. Behold, ye are all children of Israel; give here your advice and counsel.

And all the people arose as one man, saying, We will not any of us go to his tent, neither will we any of us turn into his house. But now this shall be the thing which we will do to Gibeah; we will go up by lot against it; And we will take ten men of an hundred throughout all the tribes of Israel, and an hundred of a thousand, and a thousand out of ten thousand, to fetch victual for the people, that they may do, when they come to Gibeah of Benjamin, according to all the folly that they have wrought in Israel.

So all the men of Israel were gathered against the city, knit together as one man. And the tribes of Israel sent men through all the tribe of Benjamin, saying, What wickedness is this that is done among you? Now therefore deliver us the men, the children of Belial, which are in Gibeah, that we may put them to death, and put away evil from Israel. But the children of Benjamin would not hearken to the voice of their brethren the children of Israel. But the children of Benjamin gathered themselves together out of the cities unto Gibeah, to go out to battle against the children of Israel. (*Judges* 20:1-14.)

The battle that followed was long and hard, and was almost lost, so well did this single tribe defend itself against the other eleven. Furthermore, the other tribes were guided by Jehovah himself, with the Levite priests interpreting the war commands he gave them through the oracular device known as the "~~Urim and Thummin~~." But in the end, the tribe of Benjamin was almost utterly destroyed - all but three hundred of the men were killed.

However, the victorious tribes had reason to lament. Now one of the tribes of Israel would surely become extinct! For during the war, the warriors from the eleven tribes had sworn an oath "before the Lord," in the city of ~~Mizpeh~~ (the same city where the only ~~Benjamite king of Israel, Saul~~, was first presented to the people). All of the tribesmen had sworn that they would not allow their daughters to marry Benjamite men.

> Now the men of Israel had sworn in Mizpeh, saying, There shall not any of us give his daughter unto Benjamin to wife. And the people came to the house of God, and abode there till even before God, and lifted up their voices, and wept sore; And said, O LORD God of Israel, why is this come to pass in Israel, that there should be to day one tribe lacking in Israel? And it came to pass on the morrow, that the people rose early, and built there an altar, and offered burnt offerings and peace offerings. And the children of Israel said, Who is there among all the tribes of Israel that came not up with the congregation unto the LORD? For they had made a great oath concerning him that came not up to the LORD to Mizpeh, saying, He shall surely be put to death. And the children of Israel repented them for Benjamin their brother, and said, There is one tribe cut off from Israel this day. How shall we do for wives for them that remain, seeing we have sworn by the LORD that we will not give them of our daughters to wives?

Yet there was one group among them, the "camp from Jabeshgilead" (thought to be located in the territory of Gad), who had not taken the oath. So the rest of the Israelites went and killed every man and woman, except for four hundred virgins, that they found. These they captured and sent, for some reason, to the Canaanite city of Shiloh:

> And they said, What one is there of the tribes of Israel that came not up to Mizpeh to the LORD? And, behold, there came none to the camp from Jabeshgilead to the assembly. For the people were numbered, and, behold, there were none of the inhabitants of Jabeshgilead there. And the congregation sent thither twelve thousand men of the valiantest, and commanded them, saying, Go and smite the inhabitants of Jabeshgilead with the edge of the sword, with the women and the children. And this is the thing that ye shall do, ~~Ye shall utterly destroy every male, and every woman that hath lain by man.~~ And they found among the inhabitants of Jabeshgilead four hundred young virgins, that had known no man by lying with any male: and they brought them unto the camp to Shiloh, which is in the land of Canaan. And the whole congregation sent some to speak to the children of Benjamin that were in the rock Rimmon, and to call peaceably unto them.

The Daughters of Shiloh about to be captured

They then offer the 400 virgins to the Benjamites as wives. But strangely, even though there were 400 virgins, and only 300 Benjamite men, the virgins did not "suffice." As the text states:

> And Benjamin came again at that time; and they gave them wives which they had saved alive of the women of Jabeshgilead: and yet so they sufficed them not. And the people repented them for Benjamin, because that the LORD had made a breach in the tribes of Israel. Then the elders of the congregation said, How shall we do for wives for them that remain, seeing the women are destroyed out of Benjamin? And they said, There must be an inheritance for them that be escaped of Benjamin, that a tribe be not destroyed out of Israel. Howbeit we may not give them wives of our daughters: for the children of Israel have sworn, saying, Cursed be he that giveth a wife to Benjamin.

So they then offered the Benjamites "the daughters of Shiloh":

> Then they said, Behold, there is a feast of the LORD in Shiloh yearly in a place which is on the north side of Bethel, on the east side of the highway that goeth up from Bethel to Shechem, and on the south of Lebonah. Therefore they commanded the children of Benjamin, saying, Go and lie in wait in the vineyards; And see, and, behold, if the daughters of Shiloh come out to dance in dances, then come ye out of the vineyards, and catch you every man his wife of the daughters of Shiloh, and go to the land of Benjamin.

> And it shall be, when their fathers or their brethren come unto us to complain, that we will say unto them, Be favourable unto them for our sakes: because we reserved not to each man his wife in the war: for ye did not give unto them at this time, that ye should be guilty. And the children of Benjamin did so, and took them wives, according to their

number, of them that danced, whom they caught: and they
went and returned unto their inheritance, and repaired the
cities, and dwelt in them.

There is something somewhat confusing about this story. *The Book
of Judges* is trying to convince us that the virgins from
Jabeshgilead "would not suffice," and so the Benjamites were
forced to marry women from Shiloh. And yet the narrative had
already revealed that the virgins from Jabeshgilead had just been
captured and sent to Shiloh! So in all likelihood, the girls from
Jabeshgilead that "did not suffice" were the same as the girls from
Shiloh that they married. But for some reason, the text tries to
convince us that these are two separate groups of girls.
Furthermore, the fact that the girls of Jabeshgilead were virgins,
and that the "daughters of Shiloh" were dancing in the vineyards
when the Benjamites were sent out to "catch" them, indicates an
ancient fertility rite, much like ancient pagan Easter rituals, in
which young virgins were captured and raped by young boys.

So what is *The Book of Judges* trying to indicate? That the virgins
were really from Jabeshgilead, the only Israelite town that had not
taken the oath against marrying their daughter to Benjamites; or
that they were really Canaanite virgins from Shiloh? Either way,
we are left understanding that all of the Benjamite generations that
followed were descendants of these "virgins of the vineyards."

A Royal Race of Sex Gods

The story of the war with the Benjamites, and the rape of the
concubine that preceded it, appears to contain some significant
elements in it. In substance, it is very similar to a story found in
Genesis, in which Lot is visited by two angels (or "Watchers," in
some translations). And just like the young Levite in the other
story, there is something about the angels that the townspeople of
Sodom (where Lot lived) found irresistible. They besieged the

house of Lot and demanded that the angels come out to have sex with them. As the story goes:

And there came two angels to Sodom at even; and Lot sat in the gate of Sodom: and Lot seeing them rose up to meet them; and he bowed himself with his face toward the ground; And he said, Behold now, my lords, turn in, I pray you, into your servant's house, and tarry all night, and wash your feet, and ye shall rise up early, and go on your ways. And they said, Nay; but we will abide in the street all night. And he pressed upon them greatly; and they turned in unto him, and entered into his house; and he made them a feast, and did bake unleavened bread, and they did eat.

But before they lay down, the men of the city, even the men of Sodom, compassed the house round, both old and young, all the people from every quarter: And they called unto Lot, and said unto him, Where are the men which came in to thee this night? bring them out unto us, that we may know them. And Lot went out at the door unto them, and shut the door after him, And said, I pray you, brethren, do not so wickedly. Behold now, I have two daughters which have not known man; let me, I pray you, bring them out unto you, and do ye to them as is good in your eyes: only unto these men do nothing; for therefore came they under the shadow of my roof. And they said, Stand back. And they said again, This one fellow came in to sojourn, and he will needs be a judge: now will we deal worse with thee, than with them. And they pressed sore upon the man, even Lot, and came near to break the door. But the men put forth their hand, and pulled Lot into the house to them, and shut to the door. And they smote the men that were at the door of the house with blindness, both small and great: so that they wearied themselves to find the door.

Clearly, these two stories are connected on a symbolic level. So many of the details are the same, even the fact that angels (just like the Levite and his concubine in the other story) were going to sleep in the street until Lot (like the old man in the other story) took them in. The fact that the "angels" in the Lot story are called "Watchers" in apocryphal versions of the tale indicates that these beings were indeed of the same race described as "Nephilim" or "sons of God" elsewhere in *The Book of Genesis*.

I am speaking, of course, about *Genesis 6*, in which the "sons of God" (angels) are described as coming down from Heaven to impregnate human women. This incident is greatly elaborated on in *The Book of Enoch*, and other Judeo-Christian texts. The children born of these unions were considered abominations by God, and this is what caused him to bring about the Deluge, to wipe the Earth clean of the pestilence. Different permutations of this myth can be found everywhere, in Greek, Egyptian, Indian, and Babylonian myths.

Also, different versions of the Watcher myth, or references to it, can be found throughout the Bible and other Jewish legends. An apocryphal text called *The Book of the Cave of Treasures* describes how the "sons of Seth" were lured from the Mountain of Paradise by the "daughters of Cain," and enticed into having sex with them, against the expressed wishes of God, thus bringing damnation to the race spawned from this union, and bringing about the Flood as punishment. A Gnostic text called *The Origin of the World* describes how Eve was once raped by "the Prime Ruler [God] and his Angels" while in paradise, and thus gave birth to a cursed race implied to be that of Cain and his descendants.

In each of these accounts, there is something about these angels that makes them sexually desirous to humans, even to human males, and entices them to commit obscene acts. What was it about the Watchers that made them so irresistible to the Sodomites, and what was it about the Levite that made him so irresistible to the "sons of Belial" of the tribe of Benjamin?

In *The Book of Enoch*, the Watchers are described as being breathtakingly beautiful, with pure white skin and piercing, hypnotic eyes. It was these eyes after which they were named (in Hebrew they were called "ayin" "those who watch, or see"), and the eyes themselves may have played the key role in causing these beings to seem so sexually attractive. The texts are very particular about describing how the Watchers "cast their eyes" upon the women they were about to seduce.[2] They also had enormous penises. *The Book of Enoch* says that they were consumed with lust upon the sight of human women, and as they descended from Heaven, "their parts of shame hung down like horses."

According to the website multiorgasmic.com, the Watchers were of a much higher level of sexual potency than human males, capable of having limitless orgasms without the "Male Refractory Period" (MRP) that prevents most human men from doing this. The website claims that the Watchers taught human females how to enjoy multiple orgasms as well. *The Book of Enoch* and other texts seem to back up this assertion. The Watchers were accused by God of teaching women to perform sexual abominations that they had never known of before, and of teaching them the use of make-up and jewelry, by which means these women then went about seducing other men. Thus was rampant promiscuity and fornication spread about the land.[3]

The race that was spawned by this miscegenation was described as being full of monstrous, sinful, evil creatures, but the sins they were most prone to were sexual in nature. They were called

---

[2] In the Watchers we may see the origin of notions like "the Evil Eye" and "the All-Seeing Eye.

[3] They taught the human women to use eye make-up in particular, undoubtedly to make them look more like the Watchers themselves.

"bastard," "souls addicted to lust," and "children of fornication." In the Bible, they are identified, among other words, by the term "Rephaim." Multiorgasmic.com claims that this term comes from the root word "Rapha," which they translate to mean "hard, potent, masculine, male, or virile." It also may be linked to the root of the word "rape." This links up with a Canaanite legend regarding a line of fallen kings known as "rp'um" - "Dispensers of Fertility." In addition, it may be connected to the legend of the Cainites (the descendants of Cain), who were said to have been so sexually insatiable that they kept two separate sets of wives: one for the purposes of procreation, and the other for the purposes of pleasure.

Multiorgasmic.com claims that the descendants of this race can be found today, and that they possess virility and sexual capacity beyond that of normal human males. In fact, they specifically believe that the Benjamites were among these descendants. On their website, they discuss hints that can be found in *Genesis* indicating that Benjamin, purportedly Jacob's second son by Rachel (and twelfth son in total), was actually the son of a Watcher. They point out that while the conception of each of Jacob's other children is specifically described in *Genesis*, Benjamin's conception is not. This even though Rachel's womb had been barren for decades before she bore her first son, Joseph, and then only by divine intervention - making the conception of a second son seem all the more worthy of mention. In addition, they point out that Jacob received a number of visitations from Watchers in the months preceding Benjamin's birth. On one night in particular, at a time which should have coincided with Benjamin's conception, Jacob made all of his wives and children sleep on the other side of the river while he famously wrestled with one of the angels - leaving Rachel alone and vulnerable to divine rape.

When Rachel gave birth to Benjamin, the birth was so troublesome that she named him "Benoni" ("Child of Travail") just before she

~~died of her pains.~~ Benjamin was only renamed afterwards by his "father" Jacob. The people at multiorgasmic.com believe that "Benjamin" may mean "Son of the Min" - "Min" being an Egyptian term for a mythological race that appears to be equivalent to that of the Nephilim. In any case, "Benjamin" is certainly similar to "Bene-ha-Elohim," the word translated as "sons of God" in *Genesis*. Benjamin also named his first son "Rapha," similar to "Rephaim," the Hebrew word for the human/Nephilim hybrid race.

~~If the Benjamites were truly descendants of the Nephilim, this may explain why they were considered worthy of the crown of Israel, and to be "God's anointed,"~~ even though Benjamin was the youngest of Jacob's children. Certain characteristics of the Benjamite King Saul may indicate such a parentage, namely that he was a head taller than all other Israelite men, and so beautiful that all women found him irresistible.

While the descendants of the Nephilim were clearly regarded with awe by the rest of the human population, ~~they were also clearly regarded with vehement hatred by God, who in all accounts would stop almost at nothing to destroy every remnant of their seed.~~ This genocidal impulse demonstrates itself in *Genesis 6*, when God floods the Earth to rid it of the Rephaim. The Watchers only manage to salvage the bloodline of their descendants, by saving a remnant of the population from destruction: in this case, Noah and his family.[4] Later on in *Genesis*, God destroys Sodom and Gomorrah, the inhabitants of whom, from their behavior, would appear to be Nephilim descendants. This occurs immediately after the attempted rape of the Watchers by the Sodomites outside of Lot's house. Once again, the Watchers preserve a remnant of the population - Lot's family. In the apparently related tale of the Benjamites, the tribe is almost utterly destroyed after the rape of the Levite's concubine, and the attempted rape of the Levite

---

[4] In non-Biblical accounts, it is clear that it is the Watchers, and not "God," who is responsible for saving Noah.

himself. In this case, the remnant was preserved by mating them with the "daughters of Shiloh."

The Fate of the Benjamites

There are many theories about what happened to the Benjamites after the war. The general theory is that they were subsumed into the kingdom of Judah, their descendants primarily staying in the region around Jerusalem that had been allocated to their tribe. Thus many figures in the New Testament, including Mary Magdalene, and even the Apostle Paul (who, significantly, was originally named "Saul") were from the lineage of Benjamin. Indeed, some historians affirm that virtually everyone who lived in the region of Galilee, where Jesus lived, was of this lineage. As multiorgasmic.com states:

> In fact, there is strong evidence that most if not all of Jesus' disciples were of the Tribe of Benjamin. This is due to the fact that the province known as "Galilee" belonged to the Tribe of Benjamin. Thus to be a "Galilean" was to be a Benjamite...
>
> Additionally, the cities of Nazareth (town most identified with Jesus), Capernaum (where Jesus first announced his Messianic mission), Cana (where Jesus turned water into wine... possibly at his own wedding), and Magdala (town most identified with Mary Magdalene) are all in Galilee and at that time populated predominantly by Benjamites. And of course there is the Sea of Galilee where so many other great miracles occurred.
>
> As it is well known, it was in Galilee that Jesus ostentatiously spent most of his ministry, being also identified often in scripture as "Jesus of Galilee."

It is further interesting to note that the very city of Jerusalem was originally a Benjamite city, given to the Tribe of Benjamin for their inheritance. It wasn't until the advent of King David that Jerusalem was claimed by him as his royal city and henceforth became a property of his own Tribe of Judah.

However, there is evidence that Benjamites ended up elsewhere also. As explained in *Holy Blood, Holy Grail*, by Baigent, et. al., the Priory of Sion's *Secret Dossiers* state that the Benjamites were exiled: "Their exile supposedly took them to Greece, to the central Pelopponesus - to Arcadia." The royal house of Arcadia later intermarried with the line that eventually resulted in the Merovingian kings - the Grail bloodline of Europe. *Secret Dossiers* tells us that:

> One day the descendants of Benjamin left their country; certain remained; two thousand years later, Godfroi VI [de Bouillon] became King of Jerusalem and founded the Ordre de Sion.

Holy Blood, Holy Grail adds other details that appear to tie the Benjamites in with the Merovingian kings, and with Freemasonry:

> According to Robert Graves, for example, the day sacred to Benjamin was December 23 Dagobert's feast day. Among the three clans that comprised the tribe of Benjamin there was the clan of Ahiram - which might in some obscure way pertain to Hiram, builder of the temple of Solomon and central figure in Masonic tradition. Hiram's most devoted disciple, moreover, was named Benoni, Benjamin's original name.

Indeed, there is a very good reason why Benjamin might have originally been named after Hiram of Tyre, one of Phoenicia's greatest kings. According to Michael Bradley's *Holy Grail Across the Atlantic*, the Benjamites had significant ties to the Phoenicians:

> But it came to pass that most of the Benjamites left Palestine, and this was because of a civil war among the Israelites. The Tribe of Benjamin came into conflict with the other eleven Tribes because the Benjamites were apparently allied with the 'Sons of Belial' and would not attempt to impose Israelite laws and customs upon them. This war is covered in Judges 21 in the Bible. The result was that most of the Benjamites left Palestine, or were expelled by the victorious eleven Tribes. The 'Sons of Belial' with whom the Benjamites were allied, or against whom they refused to go to war...were none other than the Phoenicians of Tyre and Sidon...

More than that, *Holy Blood, Holy Grail* seems to suggest that the Benjamites may have even considered the god known as "Belial" to literally be one of their ancestors:

> There is the legend of King Belus's son, one Danaus, who arrives in Greece, with his daughters, by ship. His daughters are said to have introduced the cult of the Mother Goddess, which became the established cult of the Arcadians. According to Robert Graves, the Danaus myth records the arrival in the Peloponnesus of 'colonists from Palestine.' Graves states that King Belus is in fact Baal, or Bel - or perhaps Belial [a form of the Mother Goddess often associated with images of a bull or calf] from the Old Testament. It is also worthy of note that one of the clans of the Tribe of Benjamin was the clan of Bela ... Indeed, it is possible that the worship of the golden calf in *Exodus* ... may have been a specifically Benjamite ritual.

The Holy Whores of Israel

It is clear from reading the Old Testament that in the eyes of the Hebrew God, the only thing worse than worshipping the gods of other, non-Israelite tribes is marrying the daughters of non-Israelite tribes. The Hebrews believed quite literally that the curses and blessings of their god Yahweh had the power to be passed on intergenerationally through patrilineal descent. They believed that a special covenant had been made between their ancestor, Abraham, and the Hebrew god which conferred an exalted status upon their people - a covenant that was confirmed later by Isaac and Jacob as well. This covenant had been sealed by the rite of circumcision, starting with Abraham, which Abraham's children, and all servants of Yahweh thereafter undertook. It was only by passing through this ordeal that a person not already of Abraham's bloodline could enter into the covenant, and then the blessings of Yahweh would be passed down through their bloodline as well. Thus could an unclean man be made clean.

But there was no such rite to bring unclean women into the covenant. Therefore, women born of uncircumcised men from non-Israelite tribes were considered unfit for marriage, because they were thought to carry within their very blood an allegiance to other gods. It is for this reason that only those born of Jewish women are themselves considered Jews. According to rabbinical tradition, this law is derived from *Deuteronomy 7:4*, forbidding the taking of non-Israelite wives, "For they will turn thy son away from following me, that they may serve other gods." Thus most marriages to foreign wives were considered illegitimate.

The children born of such marriages were thought to carry within their blood the curse of Yahweh. However, the belief in generational curses and blessings was not something unique to the Hebrews. Many elements of their early culture, including many aspects of their religion, were borrowed from the Canaanites, cousins of the Hebrew people. The Hebrews had taken part of Canaan (after many years of genocidal tribal wars) when Yahweh had directed them to seize this land. The concept that one could establish a family covenant with a deity, the blessings of which would be passed down to one's descendants, was among the elements that the Israelites picked up from their cousins.

The Bible describes the land of Canaan as being inhabited mostly by Rephaim, the offspring of the Nephilim that the Bible refers to as "giants." If the Canaanites were giants, and they were also cousins of the Hebrews, that implies that the early Hebrews were also giants, and of Nephilim descent as well. Such a proposition is bourn out by numerous Jewish legends stating that all of the Biblical patriarchs up to and including the twelve sons of Jacob were giants. It appears that the pantheon of deities that were worshipped by the Canaanites, and by other Middle Eastern tribes, in fact represented ancestral gods - the angels, or Nephilim, who helped spawn their races in antediluvian times. And among this pantheon was Yahweh, who, before becoming the patron deity of the Israelites, was seen as being part of a family of gods. The goddess Ashtoreth (reviled in the Bible) was thought by some to be his consort.

But at some point, the Israelites became convinced that they had made a special covenant with Yahweh. He was their God, they were his children, and they were not to worship other gods or goddesses, or marry women from tribes outside of the covenant. Yet many did it anyway, even beloved, heroic Biblical figures like David and Solomon. The entire royal line of Israel has been polluted numerous times by the marrying of "strange women." Inevitably, this always led to the tainted bridegrooms indulging in the worship of strange gods. Why might this be so? Why would they knowingly bring the curses of Yahweh upon themselves and their bloodline by marrying foreign women and worshipping strange gods?

The easy answer is that they thought that the foreign gods could offer them something that Yahweh couldn't. They thought that the blessings which could be obtained by allying themselves with the other gods outweighed the curses that Yahweh would inflict on them. Furthermore, if they understood these other gods to be ancestors of theirs, they may have felt they had a duty to serve them. There were undoubtedly dynastic and political advantages as well - rights and property gained through such marriages.

Issues such as these seem to be at the heart of the strange story of the Benjamites. We are led to believe from the narrative of the story that the other tribes declared war on the Benjamites because they failed to prevent the "sons of Belial" from raping the Levite's concubine, even though it was the old man that the Levite was staying with that offered her to them in the first place, and the Levite did not stop him. Closer examination reveals that behind this story lies an allegory for rape of a different sort.

According to *The Legends of the Jews, Volume 1*, by Louis Ginzberg, the real cause of the Benjamite war was spiritual. And we do see evidence of this in the text of *The Book of Judges*. For in the chapters preceding this story, *The Book of Judges* discusses how a "man of Mount Ephraim" named Micah, the son of Samson and Delilah. Those familiar with this story know that Samson was a giant, who, like the Merovingian kings, purportedly had magical powers that were derived from his long hair. He was one of the judges of Israel (before they had kings), and his arch-enemies were the Philistines. Delilah was the Philistine wife he took, who is most famous for having sold the secret of Samson's magical strength (his hair) to the Philistines for a vast cache of silver, leading to Samson's capture and then death. She then gave some of this silver to her son Micah, who forged a number of pagan idols out of it, and then hired a young Levite to be a priest to them. *Judges* states: "Then said Micah, Now know I that the Lord will do me good, seeing I have a Levite to my priest." It is not explained why Micah would think that "the Lord" (presumably Yahweh) would appreciate him worshipping idols, but it is clear that Levites were considered well-equipped for the priesthood *no matter what gods* they ministered to (ironic since it was supposedly Yahweh, who ordained them as the priestly caste in the first place).

Anyway, Micah, his Levite, and their idols apparently became well-known to all throughout the land - perhaps partially because this unidentified Levite was, according to Louis Ginzberg, the grandson of Moses. At around this time, the members of the tribe of Dan were seeking out land to occupy, "for unto that day all their inheritance had not yet fallen unto them among the tribes of Israel." They decided to seize the land of Zorah, and, as per the usual Israelite custom, annihilate the local population. On their way to war, they stop by the house of Micah. Seeking spiritual aid in their conquest of Zorah, they stole Micah's idols, and his Levite, who went with them gleefully! As *Judges* tells us:

> And these went into Micah's house, and fetched the carved image, the ephod, and the teraphim, and the molten image. Then said the priest unto them, What do ye? And they said unto him, Hold thy peace, lay thine hand upon thy mouth, and go with us, and be to us a father and a priest: is it better for thee to be a priest unto the house of one man, or that thou be a priest unto a tribe and a family in Israel? And the priest's heart was glad, and he took the ephod, and the teraphim, and the graven image, and went in the midst of the people. So they turned and departed, and put the little ones and the cattle and the carriage before them.

> And when they were a good way from the house of Micah, the men that were in the houses near to Micah's house were gathered together, and overtook the children of Dan. And they cried unto the children of Dan. And they turned their faces, and said unto Micah, What aileth thee, that thou comest with such a company? And he said, Ye have taken

away my gods which I made, and the priest, and ye are gone away: and what have I more? and what is this that ye say unto me, What aileth thee?

And the children of Dan said unto him, Let not thy voice be heard among us, lest angry fellows run upon thee, and thou lose thy life, with the lives of thy household. And the children of Dan went their way: and when Micah saw that they were too strong for him, he turned and went back unto his house. And they took the things which Micah had made, and the priest which he had, and came unto Laish, unto a people that were at quiet and secure: and they smote them with the edge of the sword, and burnt the city with fire.

And there was no deliverer, because it was far from Zidon, and they had no business with any man; and it was in the valley that lieth by Bethrehob. And they built a city, and dwelt therein. And they called the name of the city Dan, after the name of Dan their father, who was born unto Israel: howbeit the name of the city was Laish at the first.

As *The Legends of the Jews, Volume 1* tells us, the worship of Micah's idols, which was widespread, enraged Yahweh, bringing repercussions upon the tribes of Israel for generations to come. Ginzberg writes:

Especially the Benjamites distinguished themselves for their zeal in paying homage to [Micah's] idols. God therefore resolved to visit the sins of Israel and Benjamin upon them. The opportunity did not delay to come. It was not long before the Benjamites committed the outrage of Gibeah. Before the house of Bethac, a venerable old man, they imitated the disgraceful conduct of the Sodomites before the house of Lot.

The Book of Judges does not state explicitly that the young Levite who served Micah is the same Levite whose concubine was raped by the "sons of Belial." However, *The Legends of the Jews, Volume 1* certainly does. And it is this connection that brings the whole story into focus. Now we can understand what the story represents. The idol worship that was performed by Micah and his Levite was the same idol worship for which the Benjamite tribe had distinguished itself. Remember,*Holy Blood, Holy Grail* suggested that the worship of the golden calf was a "Benjamite ritual." It was probably a tradition they inherited from their friends (and most likely ancestors), the Canaanites. Now the Levites were the priestly tribe, and unlike the eleven other tribes of Israel, the Levites possessed no territory of their own. Rather, they were forbidden from owning any property at all. Instead, they were given special cities to live in throughout the territory of the other eleven tribes, and were obliged to earn their keep by performing priestly services, which members of all the other tribes were forbidden to do. Instead, each household paid 10% of its holdings to the Levites as a tithe, a tradition that goes back at least to the time of Abraham, who paid Melchizedek, the priest-king of Salem, 10% of his holdings.

It just so happens that Gibeah, in the territory of the Benjamites, was one such heretical city. Given this, it is unlikely that the Levite was just passing through Gibeah, and happened to lodge there. He was more than likely performing priestly services for the old man, and his concubine may have played an integral role in those services. In short, the rites may have had a sexual component to them. Familiar with the nature of such rituals, the "sons of Belial" among the Benjamites may have had their passion stirred by the sight of the Levite, and came demanding that they be allowed to participate.

On an allegorical level, though, there is even more to this rape. For it seems as though the Levite may have learned to worship strange gods from the Benjamites. It is likely that the Benjamites taught the Levites who served them, and perhaps those of neighboring tribes as well, to perform these rites. The rape of the concubine represents, then, the perversion of Israel's priesthood, which has always been symbolized in Jewish scripture as Yahweh's "bride." The metaphor was probably literal, too, for the Benjamites likely married the Levites' daughters, turning their sons into idolaters, carrying in their bloodlines cursed covenants with strange gods.

Thus, when they declared war on the Benjamites, the other eleven tribes swore that they would not allow their daughters to marry Benjamite men. It is likely that this was the origin of the exclusively Benjamite tradition of matrilineal (as opposed to male, or "patrilineal") inheritance of land and titles. While only three hundred Benjamite men purportedly survived, there may have been many more widows who survived, who may not have been mentioned in the scriptural record (as most women were not). Adopting this tradition allowed the Benjamite women to pass on an inheritance, and allowed the tribe to perpetuate its heritage, although in a way that may not have been entirely recognized by the eleven other tribes. Perhaps that is why the belief was allowed to flourish that all of the Benjamites had either, if men, married out of the tribe (by taking foreign wives), or, if women, married into, and melded with, the tribe of Judah. Yet it is clear that even up to the time of Jesus and afterward, many Benjamites were well aware of their heritage and were perpetuating it. It is likely that this heritage was so well-preserved only because of the tradition of matrilineal inheritance.

But it is clear that the writers of the Hebrew scriptures, and later the Christian scriptures, wished to vilify, and to blot out from history, the tribe of Benjamin. And so their men were portrayed as rapists, and their women (like Magdalene) were portrayed as whores. For the word "rape," until recently, merely meant "unlawful sex." The notion that a woman should have any say in when and with whom she has sex is modern. In ancient times, to "rape" a girl was to have sex with, or even marry her, without the consent of her family. Likewise, a "whore" could indicate anything from a street harlot, to an adulteress, to a divorced woman, or a foreign woman, or even a rape victim. All such women were considered unclean and unfit for marriage.

Thus in a sense, the tribe of Benjamin itself became personified as womanly: because of its tradition of matrilineal inheritance; because of the emasculation that it suffered during the war with the other tribes; and undoubtedly, because it practiced the worship of a goddess, as well as multiple gods. And the tribe of Benjamite was personified as a "whore" because they were thought to have perverted Israel's priesthood with such forms of worship.

Indeed, there seems to be a distinct symbolic connection in Judaic literature between whoredom and worshipping strange gods. The Old Testament often describes profligate Israelites as having "gone a whoring after other gods." It is even worth noting that the profligate priesthood of St. John's *Revelation* is described as the "Whore of Babalon." As Margaret Starbird notes, "The one underlying theme of the Hebrew scriptures - that God is the faithful Bridegroom and that his chosen symbolic 'Bride,' the community of the covenant, is unfaithful." Part of this connection undoubtedly stems from the fact that the Israelites blamed the influence of foreign women largely for the spiritual degradation of their people. Author Claudia V. Camp makes this point in her essay "Of Lineages and Levites, Sisters and Strangers: Constructing Priestly Identity in the Post-Exilic Period." In it she writes:

> In [*The Book of Numbers*], Israel 'yokes itself' to Baal of Peor by 'playing the harlot with Moabite women,' an episode whose telling itself ... combines language about wrong worship and wrong sex.

It is perhaps significant that just prior to being gang-raped by Benjamites at Gibeah, the Levite's concubine had done some whoring of her own. *Judges 19:2* states: "And his concubine played the whore against him, and went away from him unto her father's house to Bethlehemjudah, and was there four whole months." Perhaps this is why the Levite did not object when his host threw his concubine out to the "sons of Belial" to get raped in his stead.

Perhaps another reason why worshipping false gods was associated with "whoring" is that in Hebrew tradition, as in all ancient traditions, performing a priestly function was a paid job. Not only did the priests receive their tithes, but every action they performed on behalf of their clients was paid for, and there was a very important relationship between the money paid and the priestly function that was being paid for. The Hebrew scriptures stress this importance. It was not without significance that the silver which Micah used to make his idols was the same silver that had been paid to his mother Delilah (a foreign woman) for betraying her husband Samson. Delilah was an idol worshipper, and she sold the Lord's son, Samson, to an idolatrous nation, the Philistines. Symbolically, she prostituted herself. And there are even hints in *The Book of Judges* that she may have actually *been* a prostitute prior to her marriage to Samson. In Chapter 16, immediately before meeting Delilah "in the valley of Sorek," Samson visits a harlot in Gaza, and while he is with her the Philistines lie in wait to slay him. This seems to be yet another example of the Bible subtly implying that two seemingly separate characters are in fact the same character, by placing their stories next to one another in the narrative, and by revealing symbolic connections between the two. Both figuratively and, perhaps, literally, Delilah was a whore.

It was then, in a certain sense, the wages of prostitution (and of betrayal) that Micah used to make his idols of worship, and he and his Levite priest then sold indulgences from the idols to others.

This is the true basis for the notion of tithing, and of providing "seed money" for a priesthood - a notion that is currently exploited by Christian evangelists. Originally, the idea was that the idols be made from the financial sacrifices of those who worshipped them. Even the golden calf fashioned by Aaron was made from the golden jewelry of the people who worshipped it. Thus it "contained," spiritually, their covenant with Belial, the deity it represented - a covenant bought with the price of that gold, which is why Moses had them drink the gold as a punishment - to internalize the curse which Yahweh had placed upon them for worshipping the calf. This is the same sort of ritual that the Benjamites and their Levites later enacted, including Moses' own grandson.

The Legends of the Jews, Volume 1 makes it clear that the Levites were "prostituting" themselves to strange gods, but that doing so was considered an honorable way of living. Louis Ginzberg writes of the Levite, Moses' grandson, that:

> From his grandfather he had heard the rule that a man should do 'Abodah Zarah' for hire rather than be dependent upon his fellow-creatures. The meaning of 'Abodah Zarah' here naturally is 'strange,' in the sense of 'unusual' work, but he took the term in its ordinary acceptation of 'service of strange gods.'

Such rituals may have also been associated with prostitution because it did indeed involve "sacred prostitution" i.e., sex rituals. It was *literally* prostitution, too, for the services that the priestesses of these rituals performed were paid for just like any other priestly service. It is likely that the "royal wedding" of Jesus and Mary, if it was indeed an alchemical sex magic ritual, as we suspect, gained donations for their priesthood as well. In *The Chemical Wedding of Christian Rosenkreutz*, the title character must pay a token in order to gain admission to the wedding. It is in this sense that some think Mary Magdalene may have actually been a prostitute - a sacred prostitute. Such is the opinion of Nicholas de Vere, who adds that, "It is very probable ... that the so-called Rites of Venus she ritually engaged in with the Messiah have been confused with other definitions of the word venal, which pertains not only to sex, but to payment for any service or goods."

It is of interest that the color red, and the term "scarlet woman" are associated with prostitution. De Vere associates this with the fact that Magdalene was "invariably portrayed with red hair in the Renaissance masterpieces." She is also often portrayed wearing red clothes. However, the association of red hair and garments with prostitution is quite older. We can trace it back to numerous sex goddesses worshipped in the sex rites of the ancient world, who were said to have "fire-red" hair. One such figure was the Greek Pyrrha, whose name comes from the word "Pyr" - "fire." Her name stems from the association with the temple rites of fire over which she officiated as a sacred prostitute. [5] The Nephilim, by the way, are believed by some to have had red hair.

In fact, the notion of sex magic and sacred prostitution would seem to have its roots in the original "sex crime" of the Watchers, or Nephilim, mating with human women. The Israelites, and particularly the Benjamites, had many Nephilim descendants among them, and it was their ancestral spirits who constituted the "strange gods" of idol worship. These people believed that the rites they performed helped them to form covenants with their gods, and in their sex magic rituals, they believed that they communed sexually with these gods, like their ancestors had done in the past.

As we know, the interbreeding between the Nephilim and human women was condemned by Yahweh. Furthermore, the Nephilim taught their wives all manner of sexual abominations that Yahweh did not deem appropriate for them to engage in. The entire episode

---

[5] It has been theorized that this same root word "pyr" is at the root of words like "priest" and "pharaoh.

between the Nephilim and their wives can be categorized as a "sex crime," and thus can be alluded to symbolically with stories of "rape" and "prostitution." Perhaps this explains why, in addition to the sex rites already described, the same cults have often engaged in other abominations such as sodomy, as did the "sons of Belial." Such rites would have been considered an homage to the "ultimate sex crime" of the Nephilim. For the profligate Israelites, flouting the rule of Yahweh, and thus his covenant, may have been part of the point as well.

The Forbidden Union

As a descendant of Benjamin (and possibly a Benjamite princess), Mary Magdalene embodied this symbolism by default, even though there was no injunction against marrying Benjamite *women*. But there may have been something else about her that earned her a reputation as a "whore," and made her unfit for marriage in the eyes of the rabbis. There is a belief among Catholics that she was an "adulteress" - specifically that she was the same adulteress whom Jesus saved from public stoning and absolved of her sins. However, "adulteress," like "whore," is a versatile word, and would have applied to a woman who had been divorced as well. In the book *The Legend of Thomas Didymus: The Jewish Skeptic*, James Freeman Clarke suggests that Magdalene had once been one of Herod's wives, but had been divorced by him. In his version of the story, Magdalene was a high noble woman, and that was why Herod married her. But when he tired of her, he turned her out of his house, and married Herodias, the wife of his brother, making her his wife instead. According to James Freeman Clarke, it was on the grounds of Herod's previous marriage to Magdalene that John the Baptist objected to his new marriage to Herodias, and thus ended up getting beheaded. If

Magdalene had been married previously [6], this alone would have made her a "forbidden woman," although, as we shall soon demonstrate, she was probably the perfect candidate in many other ways to be Jesus' bride priestess. Jesus may have decided to go through with the marriage despite this, so as to intentionally commit a "sex crime" for ritual purposes - the sex crime that spawns a royal race, as that of the Nephilim did.

However, if this were true, John the Baptist would have objected to the marriage, as he would have believed that the marriage would bring a curse upon Jesus' royal line of descendants. (This may explain why Jesus' relationship with John turned chilly towards the end, as the Gospels seem to indicate.) So too would most other priests and rabbis, which may be one of the reasons why this community disdained Jesus so much. Even some of Jesus' own disciples may have felt that he was bringing shame to their movement by marrying Magdalene. Thus they may have chosen not to acknowledge Jesus' marriage or progeny, and to malign the memory of the Magdalene in their writings. The Roman Church followed suit later on for other reasons.

But at the same time, there were undoubtedly many advantages of Jesus and Magdalene getting together. As many authors have suggested, Mary might have been the chief royal heir of her tribe, a descendant of the first King of Israel, Saul. And although Saul's line was usurped by that of David after his death, the Lord did make promises to Saul that, in Jesus' time, had yet to be fulfilled - the promise that his seed would also provide a second king to Israel - the last king! For Jesus, connecting himself to the line of Saul may have been integral to meeting the expectations of the prophesized Messiah.

---

[6] Being a pagan priestess or having any heathen ancestors would have disqualified her as well.

God's Anointed: The History of Kingship in Israel

When the Levite priesthood became corrupted with the worship of
Micah's idols, even the high priesthood of the tabernacle, the sons
of Eli, became corrupted. They were committing abominations in
the tabernacle: eating the raw flesh of the sacrifices instead of
following Yahweh's procedure, having sex with "the women that
assembled at the door of the tabernacle" (priestesses?), and even,
through negligence, allowing the Ark of the Covenant to be stolen
by the Philistines. (It was soon restored, and Eli's sons were
killed.) Yahweh enlisted the help of the prophet Samuel, who also
became the high priest and the chief judge of the land, to bring the
Israelites back into the fold of the covenant with God. In fact,
according to *The Legends of the Jews, Volume IV*, God wanted to
annihilate the inhabitants of the world, as he had during the Flood,
because he was so angry at the Israelites, and it was only at the
pleading of Samuel that he backed down. But the people would not
submit to his authority. As *I Samuel, 8:19-20* reads:

> Nevertheless the people refused to obey the voice of
> Samuel; and they said, Nay; but we will have a king over
> us; That we also may be like all the nations; and that our
> king may judge us, and go out before us, and fight our
> battles.

So God sent Samuel a Benjamite, a "mighty man of power," for
him to anoint as king. It was only fitting, since the tribe of
Benjamin had been held responsible for the corruption of the
priesthood, and thus the nation, that a Benjamite king should be
sent to help heal the wounds caused by that corruption. And there
was no time to lose, since the Philistines were now at war with
them, and they as yet had no leader to look up to. As *I Samuel
9:16-17* states:

To morrow about this time I will send thee a man out of the
land of Benjamin, and thou shalt anoint him to be captain
over my people Israel, that he may save my people out of
the hand of the Philistines: for I have looked upon my
people, because their cry is come unto me. And when
Samuel saw Saul, the LORD said unto him, Behold the
man whom I spake to thee of! this same shall reign over my
people.

Several extraordinary things about Saul made him an interesting
choice as king. For one thing, as I have said, he bore the marks of
Nephilim descent. He was about a foot taller than other Israelite
men, and *The Legends of the Jews, Volume IV* tells us his cousin
Abner was "a giant of extraordinary size." He even successfully
wrestled the giant Goliath one day, when the giant had attempted to
steal the Tablets of the Law from within the Ark of the Covenant.
He was also strikingly beautiful, and all women were
uncontrollably attracted to him.

Another point worth noting is that many aspects of the story of
Saul's anointing seem to reflect the symbolism of the Messiah.
Recall that Jesus entered Jerusalem on the back of a donkey, to
fulfill scriptural prophecies of the Messiah, and the manner in
which he acquired this donkey was quite peculiar. As *Matthew
21:1-7* describes it:

And when they drew nigh unto Jerusalem, and were come
to Bethphage, unto the mount of Olives, then sent Jesus two
disciples, Saying unto them, Go into the village over
against you, and straightway ye shall find an ass tied, and a
colt with her: loose them, and bring them unto me. And if
any man say ought unto you, ye shall say, The Lord hath
need of them; and straightway he will send them. All this
was done, that it might be fulfilled which was spoken by
the prophet, saying, Tell ye the daughter of Sion, Behold,
thy King cometh unto thee, meek, and sitting upon an ass,

and a colt the foal of an ass. And the disciples went, and did as Jesus commanded them, And brought the ass, and the colt, and put on them their clothes, and they set him thereon.

The prophecy that Matthew was repeating was that of *Zechariah 9:9*:

Rejoice greatly, O daughter of Zion; shout, O daughter of Jerusalem: behold, thy King cometh unto thee: he is just, and having salvation; lowly, and riding upon an ass, and upon a colt the foal of an ass.

Now in the case of Saul, it was fated by God that he should be anointed king by the prophet Samuel. And he met Samuel because he was looking for his donkeys, which he had lost three days earlier. He had heard that Samuel was a prophet, and sought his help. Like the story of Jesus and his disciples finding the asses, there is something about this scenario that seems as though it was set up ahead of time. *I Samuel 9:18-21* says:

Then Saul drew near to Samuel in the gate, and said, Tell me, I pray thee, where the seer's house is. And Samuel answered Saul, and said, I am the seer: go up before me unto the high place; for ye shall eat with me to day, and to morrow I will let thee go, and will tell thee all that is in thine heart.

And as for thine asses that were lost three days ago, set not thy mind on them; for they are found.

And on whom is all the desire of Israel? Is it not on thee, and on all thy father's house?

And Saul answered and said, Am not I a Benjamite, of the smallest of the tribes of Israel? and my family the least of all the families of the tribe of Benjamin? wherefore then speakest thou so to me?

Though Saul was almost too humble to accept the honor, shortly after eating a meal with Samuel, he was anointed king, in a ceremony reminiscent of Jesus' anointing by Mary Magdalene:

> Then Samuel took a vial of oil, and poured it upon his head, and kissed him, and said, Is it not because the LORD hath anointed thee to be captain over his inheritance?

Afterwards, Samuel described to Saul the manner in which he would find his lost asses, and the description sounds somewhat similar to when Jesus told his disciples how they would find the asses upon which he would enter Jerusalem. Samuel even predicted that Saul would be met by prophets who would give him gifts (like the "wise men" who attended Jesus' birth), and that Saul would become a prophet himself. As the text states:

> When thou art departed from me to day, then thou shalt find two men by Rachel's sepulchre in the border of Benjamin at Zelzah; and they will say unto thee, The asses which thou wentest to seek are found: and, lo, thy father hath left the care of the asses, and sorroweth for you, saying, What shall I do for my son?

> Then shalt thou go on forward from thence, and thou shalt come to the plain of Tabor, and there shall meet thee three men going up to God to Bethel, one carrying three kids, and another carrying three loaves of bread, and another carrying a bottle of wine:

> And they will salute thee, and give thee two loaves of bread; which thou shalt receive of their hands. After that thou shalt come to the hill of God, where is the garrison of the Philistines: and it shall come to pass, when thou art

come thither to the city, that thou shalt meet a company of prophets coming down from the high place with a psaltery, and a tabret, and a pipe, and a harp, before them; and they shall prophesy:

- And the Spirit of the LORD will come upon thee, and thou shalt prophesy with them, and shalt be turned into another man. And let it be, when these signs are come unto thee, that thou do as occasion serve thee; for God is with thee.

When Samuel presented Saul to the people at the Benjamite city of Mizpeh, he said, "See ye him whom the Lord hath chosen, that there is none like him among all the people?" The crowd responded by proclaiming "God save the king," which is now the title of the British national anthem. The only people to object to his kingship were the "children of Belial," who said, "How shall this man save us?"

Saul went on to become a beloved king, and is credited with having unified the Israelites like never before. The conflict with the Philistines that had caused the people of Israel to beg for a king was his main concern, and Saul organized the army like never before as well. Yet for all of the effort that Yahweh went to just to enthrone Saul, he quickly gave up on the king, and removed his blessing for what seemed like trivial reasons. Basically, there were a couple of incidents in which Yahweh commanded that certain enemies of the Israelites be slaughtered, but Saul took pity on them and allowed them to live. For this, Yahweh forsook him. He afflicted Saul with "an evil spirit," and instigated his downfall, in favor of a young servant of his named David.

You see, David was the youngest son of Jesse, a descendant of Judah, and was renowned for his musical ability as a lyre player, singer and songwriter. When Saul first became afflicted with the evil spirit, and was feeling uneasy, he hired David to play the lyre in his royal palace, because it was soothing to his soul. David became a beloved friend of Saul's, whom he regarded as part of his family. David even married Saul's daughter, Michal, and became best friends with Saul's son Jonathan. But then the evil spirit caused Saul to become jealous of David. Yahweh enlisted Samuel in his plan to dethrone the line of Saul and anoint David the new king. Saul was aware of this, and the evil spirit caused Saul to want to kill David because of it.

But every time that the spirit seized him, and Saul tried to kill David, he would snap out of it just in time, and apologize for trying to kill him. Each time they would kiss and make up afterwards, and David would forgive him. But David was wary of him, and knew that he was a wanted man because he was fated to be the next king. Yet on one occasion in which Saul tried to have David killed, and David forgave him, Saul made a peculiar prophecy, and David made a peculiar promise. *I Samuel 24: 17-22* tells us:

> And he said to David, Thou art more righteous than I: for thou hast rewarded me good, whereas I have rewarded thee evil. And thou hast shewed this day how that thou hast dealt well with me: forasmuch as when the LORD had delivered me into thine hand, thou killedst me not. For if a man find his enemy, will he let him go well away? wherefore the LORD reward thee good for that thou hast done unto me this day.

> And now, behold, I know well that thou shalt surely be king, and that the kingdom of Israel shall be established in thine hand. Swear now therefore unto me by the LORD, that thou wilt not cut off my seed after me, and that thou wilt not destroy my name out of my father's house. And David sware unto Saul. And Saul went home; but David and his men gat them up unto the hold.

Thus the royal lines of Saul and David (of Benjamin and Judah) were inextricably linked forever, because of the promises that these two made to each other.

It was not long after Saul's final attempt to kill David that Saul perished during a battle with the Philistines. On that day, three of Saul's sons were killed, and Saul was so grief-stricken that he fell upon his own sword. When David was given news of this, he wept, and slew the messenger who had told him the news so gleefully, thinking David would be happy to hear it. David insisted that everyone honor Saul in his death, and mourn him.

Now this was not the end of the feud between the lines of Saul and David. The men of Judah took David as their king, while the Benjamites, along with the rest of the other Israelite tribes, took Saul's son Ishbosheth as their king. Battles raged between them for about six years, but David finally managed to capture Israel, and was anointed as their king, making Jerusalem the national capitol of the now united kingdom. He passed this kingdom on to his son Solomon.

But after Solomon's death, the kingdom split once again into the Southern kingdom of Judah, ruled by Solomon's son Rehoboam, and the Northern Kingdom of Israel, ruled by Jeroboam, a descendant of the prophet Joseph, through the line of Joseph's twin son, Ephraim. The tribe of Judah made up the bulk of the kingdom of Judah, while Jeroboam's kingdom of Israel maintained the allegiance of most of the other tribes. These initially included the Levites, although Jeroboam later removed them from their priestly offices, and most of them then moved to Judahite territory. There still remained ten tribes in the kingdom of Israel, though, since the descendants of Joseph's two twin sons, Ephraim and Manasseh, each formed separate tribes. It was from these two tribes that all of the leadership positions in Israel were filled. But unlike after Saul's death, this time the Benjamites sided with the tribe of Judah, and were loyal to the house of David. *I Kings 12:21* tells us:

"Rehoboam... assembled all of the house of Judah, with the tribe of Benjamin." It was as if the covenant between Saul and David was still affecting their descendants. This must have been the point at which the Benjamites became "subsumed" into the tribe of Judah, because from then on, they are no longer spoken of as being separate tribes.

So why did Yahweh allow the kingdom to split in this way? It was all part of his divine plan. Now although God had given up on is anointed king Saul apparently at the drop of a hat, he was not so fickle with David. Even though David's misdeeds and debauchery far exceeded that of Saul, and were only outdone by those of his son Solomon (misdeeds that included marrying foreign wives and worshipping false gods), God remained loyal to David and his bloodline. After all, he had promised David's ancestor Judah that "The scepter shall not depart from Judah, nor the lawgiver from between his feet... and unto him shall the gathering of the people be." And in *II Samuel 23*, David declared that God "hath made with me an everlasting covenant." When David was thinking of building a temple to Yahweh in Jerusalem, God spoke to his prophet Nathan:

> And it came to pass that night, that the word of the LORD
> came unto Nathan, saying, Go and tell my servant David,
> Thus saith the LORD, Shalt thou build me an house for me
> to dwell in? ... when thy days be fulfilled, and thou shalt
> sleep with thy fathers, I will set up thy seed after thee,
> which shall proceed out of thy bowels, and I will establish
> his kingdom. He shall build an house for my name, and I
> will stablish the throne of his kingdom for ever. I will be
> his father, and he shall be my son. If he commit iniquity, I
> will chasten him with the rod of men, and with the stripes
> of the children of men: But my mercy shall not depart away
> from him, as I took it from Saul, whom I put away before
> thee. And thine house and thy kingdom shall be established

for ever before thee: thy throne shall be established for
ever. (*II Samuel* 7: 4-5, 12-16)

So God had promised David's posterity a throne no matter what
sins they committed, as part of his everlasting covenant. But he did
not promise David that he would rule over *all* of the tribes of
Israel, but Judah only. Thus, when the other tribes seceded to
create the Northern Kingdom of Israel, this was punishment for the
sins of Solomon, and it was only because of Yahweh's covenant
with David that is descendants were allowed to keep even this
kingdom of Judah. In *I Kings 11:11-13*, we read:

> Wherefore the LORD said unto Solomon, Forasmuch as
> this is done of thee, and thou hast not kept my covenant and
> my statutes, which I have commanded thee, I will surely
> rend the kingdom from thee, and will give it to thy servant.
> Notwithstanding in thy days I will not do it for David thy
> father's sake: [but] I will rend it out of the hand of thy son.
> Howbeit I will not rend away all the kingdom; [but] will
> give one tribe to thy son for David my servant's sake, and
> for Jerusalem's sake which I have chosen.

Obviously, Benjamin and Judah were together considered that "one
tribe."

Eventually, in 723 B.C., the Northern Kingdom of Israel fell to the
Assyrians, and most of its inhabitants were exiled. This is how the
"ten tribes of Israel" became famously "lost." Those whose
families did eventually return for the most part had no recollection
of their family or cultural history. But the Southern Kingdom was
not immune to attack from outside forces. In 586 B.C., the
Babylonian King Nebuchadnezzar captured Jerusalem, destroyed
the temple, and took many, if not most, of the Jews into exile in
Babylon. They were finally freed by Nebuchadnezzar's grandson
Cyrus, but again, when they returned, they had lost much of their
cultural heritage and history.

The Temple of Jerusalem was rebuilt in 520 B.C., but within 200 years the land had been captured again, this time by the Greeks, and their temple was once again desecrated. The Maccabean revolt and its aftermath lead to their independence once again, creating the "state of Judea" in 142 B.C. But 80 years later, they were again captured and subjugated, this time by the expanding Roman Empire. In 20 B.C., the building of a third Temple of Jerusalem began, but this time it served a false, Hellenized priesthood backing the puppet regime of King Herod, who had been placed on the throne by the Roman Senate.

The Grafting of Vines

This is the world into which Jesus, a direct descendant of David, and rightful inheritor of his throne, was born into. It was a country not only of subjugated, enslaved people, but of a people confused by a lack of true history or heritage, and rendered impotent by having spent several generations struggling for control of their own destiny. None but the scribes among them knew anything about their history, or the details of their religion, and even among this caste there was little agreement, as evidenced by the wide range of sects and political movements that proliferated across Israel at that time. Only the Zealots - the anti-Roman militias - had any real plan of action for taking back control of the country. The rest of the Judeans, if they weren't in league with the Roman authorities, just nursed a vague wish that some "Messiah," some scion from the house of David, would come along and save them. It had been so long since the house of David had truly ruled for any length of time, that it was a bit like modern-day Britons hoping for a new king to come from the bloodline of King Arthur. But nonetheless, the Jews hoped, and many believed he would come. He would stand up to the Goliath - Rome - the same way that small young shepherd boy, David, had done, and with the flick of a wrist bring victory for Judea once again.

But it was not merely the Judeans whom Jesus wished to lead to freedom. It was all of Israel, which was at that time split up into several different areas, including Judea, Samaria, and Galilee. Many of the people who occupied these lands were descendants of the ten tribes of Israel that had seceded from Judah to form the Northern Kingdom of Israel. The land of Samaria, home of the detested Samaritans, was even named after the city of Samaria, which was once the capitol of the Northern Kingdom of Israel. These people would have had no interest in a Messiah from the house of David. Indeed, these people were awaiting a "Messiah-ben-Joseph" - a descendant of the kingly line of Ephraim, which had once ruled over the Northern Kingdom.

While there is plenty of evidence that Jesus was a descendant of David, there is no evidence that he was a descendant of Joseph. However, it is interesting to note that his father's name was Joseph, and that, like Joseph, Jesus was a prophet. But perhaps, instead of trying to be both the "Messiah-ben-Joseph" *as well as* the "Messiah-ben-Judah," Jesus attempted to bypass the need for a Messiah ben-Joseph by embracing the kingly lineage that preceded both the kingdoms of David and of Jeroboam. This lineage, of course, was that of Saul.

Saul was the only king who these people had ever truly been united under. David never really commanded the respect of the other ten tribes the way Saul had. They were on the verge of seceding the entire time, and upon the death of Solomon, took the first opportunity they had. After Saul's death, the Israelites outside of Judah all wanted to follow Saul's son, and it was only after six years of bloody civil war that they submitted to David's rule.

When the Northern tribes broke off, the Benjamites stayed with the kingdom of Judah, and eventually blended in with the tribe of Judah. Why? Because the primacy of the royal bloodline of Saul was no longer being recognized by them. But despite the enmity that had existed between Saul and David, and the competition there had been between their bloodlines, they had always respected one another - partially because the royal lines had intermarried together, and partially because both Saul and David had been "God's anointed," and mostly because they had made a covenant with each other that they would respect each other's descendants.

In addition, there had also always been a special relationship between the Benjamites and the tribes of Ephraim and Manasseh - the two tribes descended from Joseph. This was because he was the only full-blood brother of Joseph, being the only other son of Jacob's second wife, Rachel. Benjamin also had been the only one of the sons of Jacob who was not involved in the plot to sell Joseph into slavery. It was as compensation for the suffering Joseph endured at the hands of his brothers that the kingship of Israel was promised as a birthright to Joseph's sons Ephraim. It is likely that a kingly promise was also passed on to Joseph's favorite brother.

This certainly seems to be what is alluded to in *Genesis 49*. When Jacob is giving out his blessings to his sons on his deathbed, Joseph's and Benjamin's are the last two given. To Joseph, he says:

> Joseph is a fruitful bough, even a fruitful bough by a well; whose branches run over the wall: The archers have sorely grieved him, and shot at him, and hated him: But his bow abode in strength, and the arms of his hands were made strong by the hands of the mighty God of Jacob; (from thence is the shepherd, the stone of Israel:) Even by the God of thy father, who shall help thee; and by the Almighty, who shall bless thee with blessings of heaven above, blessings of the deep that lieth under, blessings of the breasts, and of the womb: The blessings of thy father have prevailed above the blessings of my progenitors unto the utmost bound of the everlasting hills: they shall be on the head of Joseph, and on the crown of the head of him that was separate from his brethren.

This is followed by a very brief word given to Benjamin:

> Benjamin shall ravin as a wolf: in the morning he shall
> devour the prey, and at night he shall divide the spoil.

The reference to Joseph as a "fruitful bough" alludes to the royal bloodline of Ephraim that issued from him. As it turns out, "Ephraim" itself means "fruitful bough." The line "The crown of the head of him that was separate from his brethren" could perhaps be a reference to the royal blessing of Benjamin, who, according to *The Legends of the Jews*, was chosen by God to be the ancestor of both the first and the last king of Israel.

The first half of God's promise for Benjamin was fulfilled by Saul. But the only way that the second half of the promise could be fulfilled would be if the last king was a result of a dynastic alliance between the royal lines of Saul and David, allowing him to reclaim the throne of Jerusalem *and* bring the old "kingdom of Israel" back into the fold. This is why a marriage between Jesus and Magdalene would have been perfect - the ideal blending of bloodlines - "the grafting of vines."

In the Priory of Sion's *Secret Dossiers*, which they published and deposited in the Bibliotheque Nationale in Paris under the author's name "Henri Lobineau," they described the Merovingian bloodline as being the result of "vine-grafting." On the surface, it looked like they were talking about viticulture, but really, they were referring to the fusing together of royal bloodlines. Grapevines had long been a symbol used in literature to denote royal bloodlines, and indeed, were used as such in the Judaic scriptures as well. In fact, there appear to be specific references in certain scriptures that allude to the royal line of Benjamin as being the "choice vine." You will recall that, when Jacob was handing out blessings to his sons, he said to Judah:

The sceptre shall not depart from Judah, nor a lawgiver from between his feet, until Shiloh come; and unto him shall the gathering of the people be.

However, this blessing was followed by these peculiar words:

Binding his foal unto the vine, and his ass's colt unto the choice vine; he washed his garments in wine, and his clothes in the blood of grapes: His eyes shall be red with wine, and his teeth white with milk.

Recall the apparent connection between Saul's anointment as king, preceded by the odd loss, and then the discovery, of his asses, and the presentation of Jesus to Jerusalem, preceded by the mysterious discovery of "an ass" and "a colt the foal of an ass. Then compare these to the line in *Genesis* about a "foal" and an "ass's colt."

Finally, compare this to the prophecy of the Messiah found in *Zechariah 9:9*. Also, recall that this prophecy was repeated and referred to in *Matthew 21:5*, when Jesus sent his disciples looking for the two asses. Obviously, there is a continuity of symbolism here that is alluding to something very specific. And it also has something to do with royal bloodlines, owing to the fact that the line in the blessing of Judah referred to the "foal" and the "ass's colt" being bound to the "vine" and the "choice vine."

The consensus among Biblical scholars links the symbols of the "foal" and the "ass's colt" to "a kingly estate." In other words, they represent royal thrones - the seat of power; the "driver's seat," as it were. Moreover, it seems to allude to the throne of a king, and the succeeding throne of his son (represented by the foal). And, it would seem, the throne of the son is even greater than that of the father. For while the father's throne is bound to the "vine," the son's throne is bound to the "choice vine." The only way in which the royal line could have become more "choice" would be by binding itself, through marriage, to another royal line of equal or greater significance. This then refers to the royal lines of Benjamin and Judah joining through Jesus and Mary Magdalene. The marriage would have made Jesus supremely qualified to be king over all of Israel, and their son would be even more so.

This then is the "grafting of vines" that lead to the Grail bloodline - to the Merovingian kings of France. This explains why Jesus' marriage to her would have been so important, and perhaps why the marriage, as well as the resulting offspring, were kept secret. It is perhaps worth noting that, according to Margaret Starbird, the word "Merovingian" means "vine of Mary."

Blessed and Cursed: The "Messianic Legacy"

In the course of my investigation into the legends surrounding Mary Magdalene, I have surmised that the reason why her marriage to Jesus was excised from the Bible was because the editors of the scriptures wished to extinguish all awareness of the bloodline descending from Jesus. The Church promoted a religious view of Jesus as the "son of God" who "died for our sins," and this view did not include him being a political figure of any sort, let alone an anti-Roman militant with a claim to the throne rivaling that of the Roman puppet Herod. Furthermore, if they admitted that Jesus had descendants, they would have to admit the existence of a group that had a much more direct claim to the continuation of Jesus' movement. The Church made sure that knowledge of this would remain hidden by eliminating any overt reference to Jesus' ancestors, marriage of descendants, and by branding Mary Magdalene as a whore. Naturally, by labeling her as such, she would be the last person to be thought of as a possible mate for the Holy One himself.

Moreover, I have learned that Mary Magdalene was most likely a royal heiress from the Benjamite line of Saul, possibly providing the perfect royal vine for Jesus to graft his Davidic inheritance onto. This would allow him to command the respect of descendants of all twelve Israelite tribes - to unite the kingdoms that had been separated for so long. As the child of both inheritances, their son would command even more respect. Thus, the prophecy of *Genesis 49:11* could be fulfilled as well as God's promise that the tribe of Benjamin would provide both the first and the last kings of Israel. Also, marrying Magdalene may have given Jesus and his heirs specific rights over the city of Jerusalem and the surrounding area, which traditionally belonged to the tribe of Benjamin. I learned that Mary Magdalene would have been the possessor of this royal inheritance because of the Benjamite custom of matrilineal inheritance, which resulted from the curse that was placed on the Benjamites after the "outrage at Gibeah" described in *The Book of Judges*.

In addition, I explored occult traditions which hold that Jesus and Mary Magdalene may have been the leaders of a royal sex magic cult, with Magdalene performing the role of "temple priestess" or "sacred prostitute." Obviously, if this were true, then the belief system that Jesus represented was well outside of mainstream Judaism. Indeed, he and Magdalene were most likely followers of strange gods, the worship of whom involved sexual magic. The wedding at Cana may have been at once both a proper marriage ceremony and a sex magic ritual, the purpose of which was to (a) unite the King of the Jews with his royal dynastic bride; (b) anoint him ritually as the king, and; (c) to ritually conceive a royal heir. Thus, the metaphor of Jesus turning water into wine may have symbolized using sex magic to "graft the vines" of two powerful royal bloodlines. I learned that Mary Magdalene's status as a Benjamite princess may have made her especially qualified to act as a sacred prostitute, as the Benjamites were associated specifically with the performance of rituals for strange gods. In Hebrew culture, such practices were equated with harlotry, and the women involved in these practices were thought of as being responsible for corrupting their husbands. This is yet another reason why Magdalene may have been seen as a "whore." Such women were viewed as "foreigners," i.e., outside of the covenant with Yahweh, and so were their children. When Israelite men married such women, it was believed that they brought onto the bloodline of their descendants the generational curses of strange gods.

This may impart yet another purpose to the marriage between Jesus and Mary Magdalene. Jesus was the qualified king of the Jews, and his son would have been the qualified king of all Israelites. But perhaps he aspired to something more than that. Perhaps he wished for his descendants to be the kings of foreign lands as well. But in order to set himself up to be king of the Jews, while at the same time setting his son up for something larger, he may have needed to simultaneously fulfill Yahweh's messianic promises, and at the same time, break his family's covenant with Yahweh. The "new covenant" had to be created - a covenant which those of gentile races could join into. He needed to break the exclusive hold that Yahweh had on his bloodline, and open it up to the blessings of other gods. Taking Mary Magdalene to wife and breeding the royal heir with her may have fulfilled this purpose.

If Mary Magdalene was indeed Jesus' wife, and indeed was the mother to his messianic heir, then the blessings and curses, the rights and inheritances that she carried in her blood were just as important as his in defining the characteristics of the Merovingian bloodline of France that descended from them. This would have especially been the case if she was a Benjamite, from a tribe practicing matrilineal inheritance. This would explain why she was so revered by the mystery cults of Southern France. But it also explains why they represented her in the form of the Black Madonna. For in the eyes of the Jewish priests of Christ's time, and in the eyes of the later Christian church. the Magdalene's marriage to Jesus would have been seen as bringing a curse upon the bloodline that descended from them. It is for this reason that the

Church insisted that the bloodline's very existence be kept secret. It is also for this reason that the initiates of the mystery cults of Southern France treasured these secrets like precious stones. The Grail is always said to be both sacred and cursed, and in the case of the Merovingian bloodline, that appears to most definitely be the case.

END

Printed in the USA
CPSIA information can be obtained
at www.ICGtesting.com
LVHW010801140724
785452LV00032B/1204